Alcyone by Archibald Lampman

Archibald Lampman was born on November 17th 1861 at Morpeth, Ontario in Canada. Perhaps the finest Canadian Poet of his time he is classed as a Confederation Poet.

When he was 6 the family moved to Gore's Landing on Rice Lake, Ontario, where young Archie started school. In 1868 he contracted rheumatic fever, which left him lame for many years and with a permanently weakened heart.

He attended Trinity College School in Port Hope, Ontario, and then to Trinity College in Toronto, Ontario and graduated in 1882. Whilst there he published many poems in the literary journal of Victoria College.

After attempting a career as a teacher he became a clerk in the Post Office Department in Ottawa, a position he held for the rest of his life.

On Sep. 3, 1887, Arhibald married Maude Emma Playter. "They had three children; Natalie Charlotte in 1892. Arnold Gesner in May 1894, but he was only to survive a few months and in 1898 Archibald Otto, was born.

A lover of camping it inspired much of his verse and helped him to become known as 'The Canadian Keats'. Most of his poems are about the Countryside and the natural world. He wrote in excess of 300 poems and all reveal and revel in his observations of life and landscape.

But his life was destined to be cut short. His health deteriorated, due in part to the death of his second son and his earlier problems caused by rheumatic fever.

On February 10th, 1899 Archibald Lampman died of a weak heart, an after-effect of his childhood rheumatic fever in Ottawa at the age of only 37.

He is buried at Beechwood Cemetery, in Ottawa, His grave is marked by a single word on his headstone "Lampman.". A nearby plaque cites his poem "In November":
The hills grow wintry white, and bleak winds moan
About the naked uplands. I alone
Am neither sad, nor shelterless, nor gray
Wrapped round with thought, content to watch and dream.

Index Of Poems

Alcyone

In the silent depth of space,
Immeasurably old, immeasurably far,
Glittering with a silver flame
Through eternity,
Rolls a great and burning star,
With a noble name,
Alcyone!

In the glorious chart of heaven
It is marked the first of seven;
'Tis a Pleiad:
And a hundred years of earth
With their long-forgotten deeds have come and gone,
Since that tiny point of light,
Once a splendour fierce and bright,
Had its birth
In the star we gaze upon.

It has travelled all that time
Thought has not a swifter flight
Through a region where no faintest gust
Of life comes ever, but the power of night
Dwells stupendous and sublime,
Limitless and void and lonely,
A region mute with age, and peopled only
With the dead and ruined dust
Of worlds that lived eternities ago.

Man! when thou dost think of this,
And what our earth and its existence is,
The half-blind toils since life began,
The little aims, the little span,
With what passion and what pride,
And what hunger fierce and wide,
Thou dost break beyond it all,
Seeking for the spirit unconfined
In the clear abyss of mind
A shelter and a peace majestical.
For what is life to thee,
Turning toward the primal light,
With that stern and silent face,
If thou canst not be
Something radiant and august as night,
Something wide as space?

Therefore with a love and gratitude divine
Thou shalt cherish in thine heart for sign
A vision of the great and burning star,
Immeasurably old, immeasurably far,
Surging forth its silver flame
Through eternity;
And thine inner heart shall ring and cry
With the music strange and high,
The grandeur of its name
Alcyone!

In March

The sun falls warm: the southern winds awake:
The air seethes upward with a steamy shiver:
Each dip of the road is now a crystal lake,
And every rut a little dancing river.
Through great soft clouds that sunder overhead
The deep sky breaks as pearly blue as summer:
Out of a cleft beside the river's bed
Flaps the black crow, the first demure newcomer.
The last seared drifts are eating fast away
With glassy tinkle into glittering laces:
Dogs lie asleep, and little children play

With tops and marbles in the sunbare places;
And I that stroll with many a thoughtful pause
Almost forget that winter ever was.

The City Of The End Of Things

Beside the pounding cataracts
Of midnight streams unknown to us
'Tis builded in the leafless tracts
And valleys huge of Tartarus.
Lurid and lofty and vast it seems;
It hath no rounded name that rings,
But I have heard it called in dreams
The City of the End of Things.

Its roofs and iron towers have grown
None knoweth how high within the night,
But in its murky streets far down
A flaming terrible and bright
Shakes all the stalking shadows there,
Across the walls, across the floors,
And shifts upon the upper air
From out a thousand furnace doors;

And all the while an awful sound
Keeps roaring on continually,
And crashes in the ceaseless round
Of a gigantic harmony.
Through its grim depths re-echoing
And all its weary height of walls,
With measured roar and iron ring,
The inhuman music lifts and falls.
Where no thing rests and no man is,
And only fire and night hold sway;
The beat, the thunder and the hiss
Cease not, and change not, night nor day.

And moving at unheard commands,
The abysses and vast fires between,
Flit figures that with clanking hands
Obey a hideous routine;
They are not flesh, they are not bone,
They see not with the human eye,
And from their iron lips is blown
A dreadful and monotonous cry;
And whoso of our mortal race
Should find that city unaware,
Lean Death would smite him face to face,
And blanch him with its venomed air:
Or caught by the terrific spell,
Each thread of memory snapt and cut,
His soul would shrivel and its shell

Go rattling like an empty nut.

It was not always so, but once,
In days that no man thinks upon,
Fair voices echoed from its stones,
The light above it leaped and shone:
Once there were multitudes of men,
That built that city in their pride,
Until its might was made, and then
They withered age by age and died.
But now of that prodigious race,
Three only in an iron tower,
Set like carved idols face to face,
Remain the masters of its power;
And at the city gate a fourth,
Gigantic and with dreadful eyes,
Sits looking toward the lightless north,
Beyond the reach of memories;
Fast rooted to the lurid floor,
A bulk that never moves a jot,
In his pale body dwells no more,
Or mind, or soul, an idiot!

But sometime in the end those three
Shall perish and their hands be still,
And with the master's touch shall flee
Their incommunicable skill.
A stillness absolute as death
Along the slacking wheels shall lie,
And, flagging at a single breath,
The fires shall moulder out and die.
The roar shall vanish at its height,
And over that tremendous town
The silence of eternal night
Shall gather close and settle down.
All its grim grandeur, tower and hall,
Shall be abandoned utterly,
And into rust and dust shall fall
From century to century;
Nor ever living thing shall grow,
Or trunk of tree, or blade of grass;
No drop shall fall, no wind shall blow,
Nor sound of any foot shall pass:
Alone of its accursèd state,
One thing the hand of Time shall spare,
For the grim Idiot at the gate
Is deathless and eternal there.

The Song Sparrow
Fair little scout, that when the iron year
Changes, and the first fleecy clouds deploy,

Comest with such a sudden burst of joy,
Lifting on winter's doomed and broken rear
That song of silvery triumph blithe and clear;
Not yet quite conscious of the happy glow,
We hungered for some surer touch, and lo!
One morning we awake, and thou art here.
And thousands of frail-stemmed hepaticas,
With their crisp leaves and pure and perfect hues,
Light sleepers, ready for the golden news,
Spring at thy note beside the forest ways
Next to thy song, the first to deck the hour
The classic lyrist and the classic flower.

Inter Vias

'Tis a land where no hurricane falls,
But the infinite azure regards
Its waters for ever, its walls
Of granite, its limitless swards;
Where the fens to their innermost pool
With the chorus of May are aring,
And the glades are wind-winnowed and cool
With perpetual spring;

Where folded and half withdrawn
The delicate wind-flowers blow,
And the bloodroot kindles at dawn
Her spiritual taper of snow;
Where the limits are met and spanned
By a waste that no husbandman tills,
And the earth-old pine forests stand
In the hollows of hills.

'Tis the land that our babies behold,
Deep gazing when none are aware;
And the great-hearted seers of old
And the poets have known it, and there
Made halt by the well-heads of truth
On their difficult pilgrimage
From the rose-ruddy gardens of youth
To the summits of age.

Now too, as of old, it is sweet
With a presence remote and serene;
Still its byways are pressed by the feet
Of the mother immortal, its queen:
The huntress whose tresses, flung free,
And her fillets of gold, upon earth,
They only have honour to see
Who are dreamers from birth.

In her calm and her beauty supreme,

They have found her at dawn or at eve,
By the marge of some motionless stream,
Or where shadows rebuild or unweave
In a murmurous alley of pine,
Looking upward in silent surprise,
A figure, slow-moving, divine,
With inscrutable eyes.

Refuge

Where swallows and wheatfields are,
O hamlet brown and still,
O river that shineth far,
By meadow, pier, and mill:

O endless sunsteeped plain,
With forests in dim blue shrouds,
And little wisps of rain,
Falling from far-off clouds:

I come from the choking air
Of passion, doubt, and strife,
With a spirit and mind laid bare
To your healing breadth of life:

O fruitful and sacred ground,
O sunlight and summer sky,
Absorb me and fold me round,
For broken and tired am I.

April Night

How deep the April night is in its noon,
The hopeful, solemn, many-murmured night!
The earth lies hushed with expectation; bright
Above the world's dark border burns the moon,
Yellow and large; from forest floorways, strewn
With flowers, and fields that tingle with new birth,
The moist smell of the unimprisoned earth
Comes up, a sigh, a haunting promise. Soon,
Ah, soon, the teeming triumph! At my feet
The river with its stately sweep and wheel
Moves on slow-motioned, luminous, grey like steel.
From fields far off whose watery hollows gleam,
Aye with blown throats that make the long hours sweet,
The sleepless toads are murmuring in their dream.

Personality

O differing human heart,
Why is it that I tremble when thine eyes,
Thy human eyes and beautiful human speech,

Draw me, and stir within my soul
That subtle ineradicable longing
For tender comradeship?
It is because I cannot all at once,
Through the half-lights and phantom-haunted mists
That separate and enshroud us life from life,
Discern the nearness or the strangeness of thy paths
Nor plumb thy depths.
I am like one that comes alone at night
To a strange stream, and by an unknown ford
Stands, and for a moment yearns and shrinks,
Being ignorant of the water, though so quiet it is,
So softly murmurous,
So silvered by the familiar moon.

To My Daughter

O little one, daughter, my dearest,
With your smiles and your beautiful curls,
And your laughter, the brightest and clearest,
O gravest and gayest of girls;

With your hands that are softer than roses,
And your lips that are lighter than flowers,
And that innocent brow that discloses
A wisdom more lovely than ours;

With your locks that encumber, or scatter
In a thousand mercurial gleams,
And those feet whose impetuous patter
I hear and remember in dreams;

With your manner of motherly duty,
When you play with your dolls and are wise;
With your wonders of speech, and the beauty
In your little imperious eyes;

When I hear you so silverly ringing
Your welcome from chamber or stair.
When you run to me, kissing and clinging,
So radiant, so rosily fair;

I bend like an ogre above you;
I bury my face in your curls;
I fold you, I clasp you, I love you.
O baby, queen-blossom of girls!

Chione

Scarcely a breath about the rocky stair
Moved, but the growing tide from verge to verge,
Heaving salt fragrance on the midnight air,

Climbed with a murmurous and fitful surge.
A hoary mist rose up and slowly sheathed
The dripping walls and portal granite-stepped,
And sank into the inner court, and crept
From column unto column thickly wreathed.

In that dead hour of darkness before dawn,
When hearts beat fainter, and the hands of death
Are strengthened, with lips white and drawn
And feverish lids and scarcely moving breath,
The hapless mother, tender Chione,
Beside the earth-cold figure of her child,
After long bursts of weeping sharp and wild
Lay broken, silent in her agony.
At first in waking horror racked and bound
She lay, and then a gradual stupor grew
About her soul and wrapped her round and round
Like death, and then she sprang to life anew
Out of a darkness clammy as the tomb;
And, touched by memory or some spirit hand,
She seemed to keep a pathway down a land
Of monstrous shadow and Cimmerian gloom.

A waste of cloudy and perpetual night
And yet there seemed a teeming presence there
Of life that gathered onward in thick flight,
Unseen, but multitudinous. Aware
Of something also on her path she was
That drew her heart forth with a tender cry.
She hurried with drooped ear and eager eye,
And called on the foul shapes to let her pass.

For down the sloping darkness far ahead
She saw a little figure slight and small,
With yearning arms and shadowy curls outspread,
Running at frightened speed; and it would fall
And rise, sobbing; and through the ghostly sleet
The cry came: 'Mother! Mother!' and she wist
The tender eyes were blinded by the mist,
And the rough stones were bruising the small feet.
And when she lifted a keen cry and clave
Forthright the gathering horror of the place,
Mad with her love and pity, a dark wave
Of clapping shadows swept about her face,
And beat her back, and when she gained her breath,
Athwart an awful vale a grizzled steam
Was rising from a mute and murky stream,
As cold and cavernous as the eye of death.

And near the ripple stood the little shade,
And many hovering ghosts drew near him, some
That seemed to peer out of the mist and fade

With eyes of soft and shadowing pity, dumb;
But others closed him round with eager sighs
And sweet insistence, striving to caress
And comfort him; but grieving none the less,
He reached her heartstrings with his tender cries.

And silently across the horrid flow,
The shapeless bark and pallid chalklike arms
Of him that oared it, dumbly to and fro,
Went gliding, and the struggling ghosts in swarms
Leaped in and passed, but myriads more behind
Crowded the dismal beaches. One might hear
A tumult of entreaty thin and clear
Rise like the whistle of a winter wind.

And still the little figure stood beside
The hideous stream, and toward the whispering prow
Held forth his tender tremulous hands, and cried,
Now to the awful ferryman, and now
To her that battled with the shades in vain.
Sometimes impending over all her sight
The spongy dark and the phantasmal flight
Of things half-shapen passed and hid the plain.

And sometimes in a gust a sort of wind
Drove by, and where its power was hurled,
She saw across the twilight, jarred and thinned,
Those gloomy meadows of the under world,
Where never sunlight was, nor grass, nor trees,
And the dim pathways from the Stygian shore,
Sombre and swart and barren, wandered o'er
By countless melancholy companies.

And farther still upon the utmost rim
Of the drear waste, whereto the roadways led,
She saw in piling outline, huge and dim,
The walled and towerèd dwellings of the dead
And the grim house of Hades. Then she broke
Once more fierce-footed through the noisome press;
But ere she reached the goal of her distress,
Her pierced heart seemed to shatter, and she woke.

It seemed as she had been entombed for years,
And came again to living with a start.
There was an awful echoing in her ears
And a great deadness pressing at her heart.
She shuddered and with terror seemed to freeze,
Lip-shrunken and wide-eyed a moment's space,
And then she touched the little lifeless face,
And kissed it, and rose up upon her knees.

And round her still the silence seemed to teem

With the foul shadows of her dream beguiled
No dream, she thought; it could not be a dream,
But her child called for her; her child, her child!
She clasped her quivering fingers white and spare,
And knelt low down, and bending her fair head
Unto the lower gods who rule the dead,
Touched them with tender homage and this prayer:

O gloomy masters of the dark demesne,
Hades, and thou whom the dread deity
Bore once from earthly Enna for his queen,
Beloved of Demeter, pale Persephone,
Grant me one boon;
'Tis not for life I pray,
Not life, but quiet death; and that soon, soon!
Loose from my soul this heavy weight of clay,
This net of useless woe.
O mournful mother, sad Persephone,
Be mindful, let me go!

How shall he journey to the dismal beach,
Or win the ear of Charon, without one
To keep him and stand by him, sure of speech?
He is so little, and has just begun
To use his feet
And speak a few small words,
And all his daily usage has been sweet
As the soft nesting ways of tender birds.
How shall he fare at all
Across that grim inhospitable land,
If I too be not by to hold his hand,
And help him if he fall?

And then before the gloomy judges set,
How shall he answer? Oh, I cannot bear
To see his tender cheeks with weeping wet,
Or hear the sobbing cry of his despair!
I could not rest,
Nor live with patient mind,
Though knowing what is fated must be best;
But surely thou art more than mortal kind,
And thou canst feel my woe,
All-pitying, all-observant, all-divine;
He is so little, mother Proserpine,
He needs me, let me go!

Thus far she prayed, and then she lost her way,
And left the half of all her heart unsaid,
And a great languor seized her, and she lay,
Soft fallen, by the little silent head.
Her numbèd lips had passed beyond control,
Her mind could neither plan nor reason more,

She saw dark waters and an unknown shore,
And the grey shadows crept about her soul.

Again through darkness on an evil land
She seemed to enter but without distress.
A little spirit led her by the hand,
And her wide heart was warm with tenderness.
Her lips, still moving, conscious of one care,
Murmured a moment in soft mother-tones,
And so fell silent. From their sombre thrones
Already the grim gods had heard her prayer.

To The Cricket

Didst thou not tease and fret me to and fro,
Sweet spirit of this summer-circled field,
With that quiet voice of thine that would not yield
Its meaning, though I mused and sought it so?
But now I am content to let it go,
To lie at length and watch the swallows pass,
As blithe and restful as this quiet grass,
Content only to listen and to know
That years shall turn, and summers yet shall shine,
And I shall lie beneath these swaying trees,
Still listening thus; haply at last to seize,
And render in some happier verse divine
That friendly, homely, haunting speech of thine,
That perfect utterance of content and ease.

The Song Of Pan

Mad with love and laden
With immortal pain,
Pan pursued a maiden
Pan, the god in vain.

For when Pan had nearly
Touched her, wild to plead,
She was gone and clearly
In her place a reed!

Long the god, unwitting,
Through the valley strayed;
Then at last, submitting,
Cut the reed, and made,

Deftly fashioned, seven
Pipes, and poured his pain
Unto earth and heaven
In a piercing strain.

So with god and poet;

Beauty lures them on,
Flies, and ere they know it
Like a wraith is gone.

Then they seek to borrow
Pleasure still from wrong,
And with smiling sorrow
Turn it to a song.

The Islet And The Palm

O gentle sister spirit, when you smile
My soul is like a lonely coral isle,
An islet shadowed by a single palm,
Ringed round with reef and foam, but inly calm.

And all day long I listen to the speech
Of wind and water on my charmèd beach:
I see far off beyond mine outer shore
The ocean flash, and hear his harmless roar.

And in the night-time when the glorious sun,
With all his life and all his light, is done,
The wind still murmurs in my slender tree,
And shakes the moonlight on the silver sea.

A Vision Of Twilight

By a void and soundless river
On the outer edge of space,
Where the body comes not ever,
But the absent dream hath place,
Stands a city, tall and quiet,
And its air is sweet and dim;
Never sound of grief or riot
Makes it mad, or makes it grim.

And the tender skies thereover
Neither sun, nor star, behold
Only dusk it hath for cover,
But a glamour soft with gold,
Through a mist of dreamier essence
Than the dew of twilight, smiles
On strange shafts and domes and crescents,
Lifting into eerie piles.

In its courts and hallowed places
Dreams of distant worlds arise,
Shadows of transfigured faces,
Glimpses of immortal eyes,
Echoes of serenest pleasure,
Notes of perfect speech that fall,

Through an air of endless leisure,
Marvellously musical.

And I wander there at even,
Sometimes when my heart is clear,
When a wider round of heaven
And a vaster world are near,
When from many a shadow steeple
Sounds of dreamy bells begin,
And I love the gentle people
That my spirit finds therein.

Men of a diviner making
Than the sons of pride and strife,
Quick with love and pity, breaking
From a knowledge old as life;
Women of a spiritual rareness,
Whom old passion and old woe
Moulded to a slenderer fairness
Than the dearest shapes we know.

In its domed and towered centre
Lies a garden wide and fair,
Open for the soul to enter,
And the watchful townsmen there
Greet the stranger gloomed and fretting
From this world of stormy hands,
With a look that deals forgetting
And a touch that understands.

For they see with power, not borrowed
From a record taught or told,
But they loved and laughed and sorrowed
In a thousand worlds of old;
Now they rest and dream for ever,
And with hearts serene and whole
See the struggle, the old fever,
Clear as on a painted scroll.

Wandering by that grey and solemn
Water, with its ghostly quays
Vistas of vast arch and column,
Shadowed by unearthly trees
Biddings of sweet power compel me,
And I go with bated breath,
Listening to the tales they tell me,
Parables of Life and Death.

In a tongue that once was spoken,
Ere the world was cooled by Time,
When the spirit flowed unbroken
Through the flesh, and the Sublime

Made the eyes of men far-seeing,
And their souls as pure as rain,
They declare the ends of being,
And the sacred need of pain.

For they know the sweetest reasons
For the products most malign
They can tell the paths and seasons
Of the farthest suns that shine.
How the moth-wing's iridescence
By an inward plan was wrought,
And they read me curious lessons
In the secret ways of thought.

When day turns, and over heaven
To the balmy western verge
Sail the victor fleets of even,
And the pilot stars emerge,
Then my city rounds and rises,
Like a vapour formed afar,
And its sudden girth surprises,
And its shadowy gates unbar.

Dreamy crowds are moving yonder
In a faint and phantom blue;
Through the dusk I lean, and wonder
If their winsome shapes are true;
But in veiling indecision
Come my questions back again
Which is real? The fleeting vision?
Or the fleeting world of men?

Evening
From upland slopes I see the cows file by,
Lowing, great-chested, down the homeward trail,
By dusking fields and meadows shining pale
With moon-tipped dandelions. Flickering high,
A peevish night-hawk in the western sky
Beats up into the lucent solitudes,
Or drops with griding wing. The stilly woods
Grow dark and deep and gloom mysteriously.
Cool night-winds creep, and whisper in mine ear
The homely cricket gossips at my feet.
From far-off pools and wastes of reeds I hear,
Clear and soft-piped, the chanting frogs break sweet
In full Pandean chorus. One by one
Shine out the stars, and the great night comes on.

The Clearer Self
Before me grew the human soul,

And after I am dead and gone,
Through grades of effort and control
The marvellous work shall still go on.

Each mortal in his little span
Hath only lived, if he have shown
What greatness there can be in man
Above the measured and the known;

How through the ancient layers of night,
In gradual victory secure,
Grows ever with increasing light
The Energy serene and pure:

The Soul, that from a monstrous past,
From age to age, from hour to hour,
Feels upward to some height at last
Of unimagined grace and power.

Though yet the sacred fire be dull,
In folds of thwarting matter furled,
Ere death be nigh, while life is full,
O Master Spirit of the world,

Grant me to know, to seek, to find,
In some small measure though it be,
Emerging from the waste and blind,
The clearer self, the grander me!

To The Prophetic Soul
What are these bustlers at the gate
Of now or yesterday,
These playthings in the hand of Fate,
That pass, and point no way;

These clinging bubbles whose mock fires
For ever dance and gleam,
Vain foam that gathers and expires
Upon the world's dark stream;

These gropers betwixt right and wrong,
That seek an unknown goal,
Most ignorant, when they seem most strong;
What are they, then, O Soul,

That thou shouldst covet overmuch
A tenderer range of heart,
And yet at every dreamed-of touch
So tremulously start?

Thou with that hatred ever new

Of the world's base control,
That vision of the large and true,
That quickness of the soul;

Nay, for they are not of thy kind,
But in a rarer clay
God dowered thee with an alien mind;
Thou canst not be as they.

Be strong therefore; resume thy load,
And forward stone by stone
Go singing, though the glorious road
Thou travellest alone.

The Land Of Pallas

Methought I journeyed along ways that led for ever
Throughout a happy land where strife and care were dead,
And life went by me flowing like a placid river
Past sandy eyots where the shifting shoals make head.

A land where beauty dwelt supreme, and right, the donor
Of peaceful days; a land of equal gifts and deeds,
Of limitless fair fields and plenty had with honour;
A land of kindly tillage and untroubled meads,

Of gardens, and great fields, and dreaming rose-wreathed alleys,
Wherein at dawn and dusk the vesper sparrows sang;
Of cities set far off on hills down vista'd valleys,
And floods so vast and old, men wist not whence they sprang,

Of groves, and forest depths, and fountains softly welling,
And roads that ran soft-shadowed past the open doors,
Of mighty palaces and many a lofty dwelling,
Where all men entered and no master trod their floors.

A land of lovely speech, where every tone was fashioned
By generations of emotion high and sweet,
Of thought and deed and bearing lofty and impassioned;
A land of golden calm, grave forms, and fretless feet.

And every mode and saying of that land gave token
Of limits where no death or evil fortune fell,
And men lived out long lives in proud content unbroken,
For there no man was rich, none poor, but all were well.

And all the earth was common, and no base contriving
Of money of coined gold was needed there or known,
But all men wrought together without greed or striving,
And all the store of all to each man was his own.

From all that busy land, grey town, and peaceful village,

Where never jar was heard, nor wail, nor cry of strife,
From every laden stream and all the fields of tillage,
Arose the murmur and the kindly hum of life.

At morning to the fields came forth the men, each neighbour
Hand linked to other, crowned, with wreaths upon their hair,
And all day long with joy they gave their hands to labour,
Moving at will, unhastened, each man to his share.

At noon the women came, the tall fair women, bearing
Baskets of wicker in their ample hands for each,
And learned the day's brief tale, and how the fields were faring,
And blessed them with their lofty beauty and blithe speech.

And when the great day's toil was over, and the shadows
Grew with the flocking stars, the sound of festival
Rose in each city square, and all the country meadows,
Palace, and paven court, and every rustic hall.

Beside smooth streams, where alleys and green gardens meeting
Ran downward to the flood with marble steps, a throng
Came forth of all the folk, at even, gaily greeting,
With echo of sweet converse, jest, and stately song.

In all their great fair cities there was neither seeking
For power of gold, nor greed of lust, nor desperate pain
Of multitudes that starve, or, in hoarse anger breaking,
Beat at the doors of princes, break and fall in vain.

But all the children of that peaceful land, like brothers,
Lofty of spirit, wise, and ever set to learn
The chart of neighbouring souls, the bent and need of others,
Thought only of good deeds, sweet speech, and just return.

And there there was no prison, power of arms, nor palace,
Where prince or judge held sway, for none was needed there;
Long ages since the very names of fraud and malice
Had vanished from men's tongues, and died from all men's care.

And there there were no bonds of contract, deed, or marriage,
No oath, nor any form, to make the word more sure,
For no man dreamed of hurt, dishonour, or miscarriage,
Where every thought was truth, and every heart was pure.

There were no castes of rich or poor, of slave or master,
Where all were brothers, and the curse of gold was dead,
But all that wise fair race to kindlier ends and vaster
Moved on together with the same majestic tread.

And all the men and women of that land were fairer
Than even the mightiest of our meaner race can be;
The men like gentle children, great of limb, yet rarer

For wisdom and high thought, like kings for majesty.

And all the women through great ages of bright living,
Grown goodlier of stature, strong, and subtly wise,
Stood equal with the men, calm counsellors, ever giving
The fire and succour of proud faith and dauntless eyes.

And as I journeyed in that land I reached a ruin,
The gateway of a lonely and secluded waste,
A phantom of forgotten time and ancient doing,
Eaten by age and violence, crumbled and defaced.

On its grim outer walls the ancient world's sad glories
Were recorded in fire; upon its inner stone,
Drawn by dead hands, I saw, in tales and tragic stories,
The woe and sickness of an age of fear made known.

And lo, in that grey storehouse, fallen to dust and rotten,
Lay piled the traps and engines of forgotten greed,
The tomes of codes and canons, long disused, forgotten,
The robes and sacred books of many a vanished creed.

An old grave man I found, white-haired and gently spoken,
Who, as I questioned, answered with a smile benign,
'Long years have come and gone since these poor gauds were broken,
Broken and banished from a life made more divine.

'But still we keep them stored as once our sires deemed fitting,
The symbol of dark days and lives remote and strange,
Lest o'er the minds of any there should come unwitting
The thought of some new order and the lust of change.

'If any grow disturbed, we bring them gently hither,
To read the world's grim record and the sombre lore
Massed in these pitiless vaults, and they returning thither,
Bear with them quieter thoughts, and make for change no more.'

And thence I journeyed on by one broad way that bore me
Out of that waste, and as I passed by tower and town
I saw amid the limitless plain far out before me
A long low mountain, blue as beryl, and its crown

Was capped by marble roofs that shone like snow for whiteness,
Its foot was deep in gardens, and that blossoming plain
Seemed in the radiant shower of its majestic brightness
A land for gods to dwell in, free from care and pain.

And to and forth from that fair mountain like a river
Ran many a dim grey road, and on them I could see
A multitude of stately forms that seemed for ever
Going and coming in bright bands; and near to me

Was one that in his journey seemed to dream and linger,
Walking at whiles with kingly step, then standing still,
And him I met and asked him, pointing with my finger,
The meaning of the palace and the lofty hill.

Whereto the dreamer: 'Art thou of this land, my brother,
And knowest not the mountain and its crest of walls,
Where dwells the priestless worship of the all-wise mother?
That is the hill of Pallas; those her marble halls!

'There dwell the lords of knowledge and of thought increasing,
And they whom insight and the gleams of song uplift;
And thence as by a hundred conduits flows unceasing
The spring of power and beauty, an eternal gift.'

Still I passed on until I reached at length, not knowing
Whither the tangled and diverging paths might lead,
A land of baser men, whose coming and whose going
Were urged by fear, and hunger, and the curse of greed.

I saw the proud and fortunate go by me, faring
In fatness and fine robes, the poor oppressed and slow,
The faces of bowed men, and piteous women bearing
The burden of perpetual sorrow and the stamp of woe.

And tides of deep solicitude and wondering pity
Possessed me, and with eager and uplifted hands
I drew the crowd about me in a mighty city,
And taught the message of those other kindlier lands.

I preached the rule of Faith and brotherly Communion,
The law of Peace and Beauty and the death of Strife,
And painted in great words the horror of disunion,
The vainness of self-worship, and the waste of life.

I preached, but fruitlessly; the powerful from their stations
Rebuked me as an anarch, envious and bad,
And they that served them with lean hands and bitter patience
Smiled only out of hollow orbs, and deemed me mad.

And still I preached, and wrought, and still I bore my message,
For well I knew that on and upward without cease
The spirit works for ever, and by Faith and Presage
That somehow yet the end of human life is Peace.

Among The Orchards
Already in the dew-wrapped vineyards dry
Dense weights of heat press down. The large bright drops
Shrink in the leaves. From dark acacia tops
The nuthatch flings his short reiterate cry;
And ever as the sun mounts hot and high

Thin voices crowd the grass. In soft long strokes
The wind goes murmuring through the mountain oaks.
Faint wefts creep out along the blue and die.
I hear far in among the motionless trees
Shadows that sleep upon the shaven sod
The thud of dropping apples. Reach on reach
Stretch plots of perfumed orchard, where the bees
Murmur among the full-fringed golden-rod,
Or cling half-drunken to the rotting peach.

The Poet's Song
I
There came no change from week to week
On all the land, but all one way,
Like ghosts that cannot touch nor speak,
Day followed day.

Within the palace court the rounds
Of glare and shadow, day and night,
Went ever with the same dull sounds,
The same dull flight:

The motion of slow forms of state,
The far-off murmur of the street,
The din of couriers at the gate,
Half-mad with heat;

Sometimes a distant shout of boys
At play upon the terrace walk,
The shutting of great doors, and noise
Of muttered talk.

In one red corner of the wall,
That fronted with its granite stain
The town, the palms, and, beyond all,
The burning plain,

As listless as the hour, alone,
The poet by his broken lute
Sat like a figure in the stone,
Dark-browed and mute.

He saw the heat on the thin grass
Fall till it withered joint by joint,
The shadow on the dial pass
From point to point.

He saw the midnight bright and bare
Fill with its quietude of stars
The silence that no human prayer
Attains or mars.

He heard the hours divide, and still
The sentry on the outer wall
Make the night wearier with his shrill
Monotonous call.

He watched the lizard where it lay,
Impassive as the watcher's face;
And only once in the long day
It changed its place.

Sometimes with clank of hoofs and cries
The noon through all its trance was stirred;
The poet sat with half-shut eyes,
Nor saw, nor heard.

And once across the heated close
Light laughter in a silver shower
Fell from fair lips: the poet rose
And cursed the hour.

Men paled and sickened; half in fear,
There came to him at dusk of eve
One who but murmured in his ear
And plucked his sleeve:

'The king is filled with irks, distressed,
And bids thee hasten to his side;
For thou alone canst give him rest.'
The poet cried:

'Go, show the king this broken lute!
Even as it is, so am I!
The tree is perished to its root,
The fountain dry.

'What seeks he of the leafless tree,
The broken lute, the empty spring?
Yea, tho' he give his crown to me,
I cannot sing!'

II
That night there came from either hand
A sense of change upon the land;
A brooding stillness rustled through
With creeping winds that hardly blew;
A shadow from the looming west,
A stir of leaves, a dim unrest;
It seemed as if a spell had broke.

And then the poet turned and woke
As from the darkness of a dream,

And with a smile divine supreme
Drew up his mantle fold on fold,
And strung his lute with strings of gold,
And bound the sandals to his feet,
And strode into the darkling street.

Through crowds of murmuring men he hied,
With working lips and swinging stride,
And gleaming eyes and brow bent down;
Out of the great gate of the town
He hastened ever and passed on,
And ere the darkness came, was gone,
A mote beyond the western swell.

And then the storm arose and fell
From wheeling shadows black with rain
That drowned the hills and strode the plain;
Round the grim mountain-heads it passed,
Down whistling valleys blast on blast,
Surged in upon the snapping trees,
And swept the shuddering villages.

That night, when the fierce hours grew long,
Once more the monarch, old and grey,
Called for the poet and his song,
And called in vain. But far away,
By the wild mountain-gorges, stirred,
The shepherds in their watches heard,
Above the torrent's charge and clang,
The cleaving chant of one that sang.

A Thunderstorm
A moment the wild swallows like a flight
Of withered gust-caught leaves, serenely high,
Toss in the windrack up the muttering sky.
The leaves hang still. Above the weird twilight,
The hurrying centres of the storm unite
And spreading with huge trunk and rolling fringe,
Each wheeled upon its own tremendous hinge
Tower darkening on. And now from heaven's height
With the long roar of elm-trees swept and swayed,
And pelted waters, on the vanished plain
Plunges the blast. Behind the wild white flash
That splits abroad the pealing thunder-crash,
Over bleared fields and gardens disarrayed,
Column on column comes the drenching rain.

The City
Canst thou not rest, O city,
That liest so wide and fair;

Shall never an hour bring pity,
Nor end be found for care?

Thy walls are high in heaven,
Thy streets are gay and wide,
Beneath thy towers at even
The dreamy waters glide.

Thou art fair as the hills at morning,
And the sunshine loveth thee,
But its light is a gloom of warning
On a soul no longer free.

The curses of gold are about thee,
And thy sorrow deepeneth still;
One madness within and without thee,
One battle blind and shrill.

I see the crowds for ever
Go by with hurrying feet;
Through doors that darken never
I hear the engines beat.

Through days and nights that follow
The hidden mill-wheel strains;
In the midnight's windy hollow
I hear the roar of trains.

And still the day fulfilleth,
And still the night goes round,
And the guest-hall boometh and shrilleth,
With the dance's mocking sound.

In chambers of gold elysian,
The cymbals clash and clang,
But the days are gone like a vision
When the people wrought and sang.

And toil hath fear for neighbour,
Where singing lips are dumb,
And life is one long labour,
Till death or freedom come.

Ah! the crowds that for ever are flowing
They neither laugh nor weep
I see them coming and going,
Like things that move in sleep:

Grey sires and burdened brothers,
The old, the young, the fair,
Wan cheeks of pallid mothers,
And the girls with golden hair.

Care sits in many a fashion,
Grown grey on many a head,
And lips are turned to ashen
Whose years have right to red.

Canst thou not rest, O city,
That liest so wide, so fair;
Shalt never an hour bring pity,
Nor end be found for care?

Sapphics

Clothed in splendour, beautifully sad and silent,
Comes the autumn over the woods and highlands,
Golden, rose-red, full of divine remembrance,
Full of foreboding.

Soon the maples, soon will the glowing birches,
Stripped of all that summer and love had dowered them,
Dream, sad-limbed, beholding their pomp and treasure
Ruthlessly scattered:

Yet they quail not: Winter with wind and iron
Comes and finds them silent and uncomplaining,
Finds them tameless, beautiful still and gracious,
Gravely enduring.

Me too changes, bitter and full of evil,
Dream by dream have plundered and left me naked,
Grey with sorrow. Even the days before me
Fade into twilight,

Mute and barren. Yet will I keep my spirit
Clear and valiant, brother to these my noble
Elms and maples, utterly grave and fearless,
Grandly ungrieving.

Brief the span is, counting the years of mortals,
Strange and sad; it passes, and then the bright earth,
Careless mother, gleaming with gold and azure,
Lovely with blossoms

Shining white anemones, mixed with roses,
Daisies mild-eyed, grasses and honeyed clover
You, and me, and all of us, met and equal,
Softly shall cover.

Voices Of Earth

We have not heard the music of the spheres,
The song of star to star, but there are sounds

More deep than human joy and human tears,
That Nature uses in her common rounds;
The fall of streams, the cry of winds that strain
The oak, the roaring of the sea's surge, might
Of thunder breaking afar off, or rain
That falls by minutes in the summer night.
These are the voices of earth's secret soul,
Uttering the mystery from which she came.
To him who hears them grief beyond control,
Or joy inscrutable without a name,
Wakes in his heart thoughts bedded there, impearled,
Before the birth and making of the world.

Peccavi, Domine
O Power to whom this earthly clime
Is but an atom in the whole,
O Poet-heart of Space and Time,
O Maker and Immortal Soul,
Within whose glowing rings are bound,
Out of whose sleepless heart had birth
The cloudy blue, the starry round,
And this small miracle of earth:

Who liv'st in every living thing,
And all things are thy script and chart,
Who rid'st upon the eagle's wing,
And yearnest in the human heart;
O Riddle with a single clue,
Love, deathless, protean, secure,
The ever old, the ever new,
O Energy, serene and pure.

Thou, who art also part of me,
Whose glory I have sometime seen,
O Vision of the Ought-to-be,
O Memory of the Might-have-been,
I have had glimpses of thy way,
And moved with winds and walked with stars,
But, weary, I have fallen astray,
And, wounded, who shall count my scars?

O Master, all my strength is gone;
Unto the very earth I bow;
I have no light to lead me on;
With aching heart and burning brow,
I lie as one that travaileth
In sorrow more than he can bear;
I sit in darkness as of death,
And scatter dust upon my hair.

The God within my soul hath slept,

And I have shamed the nobler rule;
O Master, I have whined and crept;
O Spirit, I have played the fool.
Like him of old upon whose head
His follies hung in dark arrears,
I groan and travail in my bed,
And water it with bitter tears.

I stand upon thy mountain-heads,
And gaze until mine eyes are dim;
The golden morning glows and spreads;
The hoary vapours break and swim.
I see thy blossoming fields, divine,
Thy shining clouds, thy blessed trees
And then that broken soul of mine
How much less beautiful than these!

O Spirit, passionless, but kind,
Is there in all the world, I cry,
Another one so base and blind,
Another one so weak as I?
O Power, unchangeable, but just,
Impute this one good thing to me,
I sink my spirit to the dust
In utter dumb humility.

An Ode To The Hills
'I will lift up mine eyes unto the hills, from whence
cometh my help.' PSALM CXXI. 1.

Æons ago ye were,
Before the struggling changeful race of man
Wrought into being, ere the tragic stir
Of human toil and deep desire began:
So shall ye still remain,
Lords of an elder and immutable race,
When many a broad metropolis of the plain,
Or thronging port by some renownèd shore,
Is sunk in nameless ruin, and its place
Recalled no more.

Empires have come and gone,
And glorious cities fallen in their prime;
Divine, far-echoing, names once writ in stone
Have vanished in the dust and void of time;
But ye, firm-set, secure,
Like Treasure in the hardness of God's palm,
Are yet the same for ever; ye endure
By virtue of an old slow-ripening word,
In your grey majesty and sovereign calm,
Untouched, unstirred.

Tempest and thunderstroke,
With whirlwinds dipped in midnight at the core,
Have torn strange furrows through your forest cloak,
And made your hollow gorges clash and roar,
And scarred your brows in vain.
Around your barren heads and granite steeps
Tempestuous grey battalions of the rain
Charge and recharge, across the plateaued floors,
Drenching the serried pines; and the hail sweeps
Your pitiless scaurs.

The long midsummer heat
Chars the thin leafage of your rocks in fire:
Autumn with windy robe and ruinous feet
On your wide forests wreaks his fell desire,
Heaping in barbarous wreck
The treasure of your sweet and prosperous days;
And lastly the grim tyrant, at whose beck
Channels are turned to stone and tempests wheel,
On brow and breast and shining shoulder lays
His hand of steel.

And yet not harsh alone,
Nor wild, nor bitter are your destinies,
O fair and sweet, for all your heart of stone,
Who gather beauty round your Titan knees,
As the lens gathers light.
The dawn gleams rosy on your splendid brows,
The sun at noonday folds you in his might,
And swathes your forehead at his going down,
Last leaving, where he first in pride bestows,
His golden crown.

In unregarded glooms,
Where hardly shall a human footstep pass,
Myriads of ferns and soft maianthemums,
Or lily-breathing slender pyrolas
Distil their hearts for you.
Far in your pine-clad fastnesses ye keep
Coverts the lonely thrush shall wander through,
With echoes that seem ever to recede,
Touching from pine to pine, from steep to steep,
His ghostly reed.

The fierce things of the wild
Find food and shelter in your tenantless rocks,
The eagle on whose wings the dawn hath smiled,
The loon, the wild-cat, and the bright-eyed fox;
For far away indeed
Are all the ominous noises of mankind,
The slaughterer's malice and the trader's greed:

Your rugged haunts endure no slavery:
No treacherous hand is there to crush or bind,
But all are free.

Therefore out of the stir
Of cities and the ever-thickening press
The poet and the worn philosopher
To your bare peaks and radiant loneliness
Escape, and breathe once more
The wind of the Eternal: that clear mood,
Which Nature and the elder ages bore,
Lends them new courage and a second prime,
At rest upon the cool infinitude
Of Space and Time.

The mists of troublous days,
The horror of fierce hands and fraudful lips,
The blindness gathered in Life's aimless ways
Fade from them, and the kind Earth-spirit strips
The bandage from their eyes,
Touches their hearts and bids them feel and see;
Beauty and Knowledge with that rare apprise
Pour over them from some divine abode,
Falling as in a flood of memory,
The bliss of God.

I too perchance some day,
When Love and Life have fallen far apart,
Shall slip the yoke and seek your upward way
And make my dwelling in your changeless heart;
And there in some quiet glade,
Some virgin plot of turf, some innermost dell,
Pure with cool water and inviolate shade,
I'll build a blameless altar to the dear
And kindly gods who guard your haunts so well
From hurt or fear.

There I will dream day-long,
And honour them in many sacred ways,
With hushèd melody and uttered song,
And golden meditation and with praise.
I'll touch them with a prayer,
To clothe my spirit as your might is clad
With all things bountiful, divine, and fair,
Yet inwardly to make me hard and true,
Wide-seeing, passionless, immutably glad,
And strong like you.

Indian Summer
The old grey year is near his term in sooth,
And now with backward eye and soft-laid palm

Awakens to a golden dream of youth,
A second childhood lovely and most calm,
And the smooth hour about his misty head
An awning of enchanted splendour weaves,
Of maples, amber, purple and rose-red,
And droop-limbed elms down-dropping golden leaves.
With still half-fallen lids he sits and dreams
Far in a hollow of the sunlit wood,
Lulled by the murmur of thin-threading streams,
Nor sees the polar armies overflood
The darkening barriers of the hills, nor hears
The north-wind ringing with a thousand spears.

Good Speech

Think not, because thine inmost heart means well,
Thou hast the freedom of rude speech: sweet words
Are like the voices of returning birds
Filling the soul with summer, or a bell
That calls the weary and the sick to prayer.
Even as thy thought, so let thy speech be fair.

The Better Day

Harsh thoughts, blind angers, and fierce hands,
That keep this restless world at strife,
Mean passions that, like choking sands,
Perplex the stream of life,

Pride and hot envy and cold greed,
The cankers of the loftier will,
What if ye triumph, and yet bleed?
Ah, can ye not be still?

Oh, shall there be no space, no time,
No century of weal in store,
No freehold in a nobler clime,
Where men shall strive no more?

Where every motion of the heart
Shall serve the spirit's master-call,
Where self shall be the unseen part,
And human kindness all?

Or shall we but by fits and gleams
Sink satisfied, and cease to rave,
Find love but in the rest of dreams,
And peace but in the grave?

White Pansies

Day and night pass over, rounding,

Star and cloud and sun,
Things of drift and shadow, empty
Of my dearest one.

Soft as slumber was my baby,
Beaming bright and sweet;
Daintier than bloom or jewel
Were his hands and feet.

He was mine, mine all, mine only,
Mine and his the debt;
Earth and Life and Time are changers;
I shall not forget.

Pansies for my dear one - heartsease
Set them gently so;
For his stainless lips and forehead,
Pansies white as snow.

Would that in the flower-grown little
Grave they dug so deep,
I might rest beside him, dreamless,
Smile no more, nor weep.

We Too Shall Sleep

Not, not for thee,
Beloved child, the burning grasp of life
Shall bruise the tender soul. The noise, and strife,
And clamour of midday thou shall not see;
But wrapt for ever in thy quiet grave,
Too little to have known the earthly lot,
Time's clashing hosts above thine innocent head,
Wave upon wave,
Shall break, or pass as with an army's tread,
And harm thee not.

A few short years
We of the living flesh and restless brain
Shall plumb the deeps of life and know the strain,
The fleeting gleams of joy, the fruitless tears;
And then at last when all is touched and tried,
Our own immutable night shall fall, and deep
In the same silent plot, O little friend,
Side by thy side,
In peace that changeth not, nor knoweth end,
We too shall sleep.

The Autumn Waste

There is no break in all the wide grey sky,
Nor light on any field, and the wind grieves,

And talks of death. Where cold grey waters lie
Round greyer stones, and the new-fallen leaves
Heap the chill hollows of the naked woods,
A lisping moan, an inarticulate cry,
Creeps far among the charnel solitudes,
Numbing the waste with mindless misery.
In these bare paths, these melancholy lands,
What dream, or flesh, could ever have been young?
What lovers have gone forth with linkèd hands?
What flowers could ever have bloomed, what birds have sung?
Life, hopes, and human things seem wrapped away,
With shrouds and spectres, in one long decay.

Vivia Perpetua
Now being on the eve of death, discharged
From every mortal hope and earthly care,
I questioned how my soul might best employ
This hand, and this still wakeful flame of mind,
In the brief hours yet left me for their use;
Wherefore have I bethought me of my friend,
Of you, Philarchus, and your company,
Yet wavering in the faith and unconfirmed;
Perchance that I may break into thine heart
Some sorrowful channel for the love divine,
I make this simple record of our proof
In diverse sufferings for the name of Christ,
Whereof the end already for the most
Is death this day with steadfast faith endured.

We were in prison many days, close-pent
In the black lower dungeon, housed with thieves
And murderers and divers evil men;
So foul a pressure, we had almost died,
Even there, in struggle for the breath of life
Amid the stench and unendurable heat;
Nor could we find each other save by voice
Or touch, to know that we were yet alive,
So terrible was the darkness. Yea, 'twas hard
To keep the sacred courage in our hearts,
When all was blind with that unchanging night,
And foul with death, and on our ears the taunts
And ribald curses of the soldiery
Fell mingled with the prisoners' cries, a load
Sharper to bear, more bitter than their blows.
At first, what with that dread of our abode,
Our sudden apprehension, and the threats
Ringing perpetually in our ears, we lost
The living fire of faith, and like poor hinds
Would have denied our Lord and fallen away.
Even Perpetua, whose joyous faith
Was in the later holier days to be

The stay and comfort of our weaker ones,
Was silent for long whiles. Perchance she shrank
In the mere sickness of the flesh, confused
And shaken by our new and horrible plight
The tender flesh, untempered and untried,
Not quickened yet nor mastered by the soul;
For she was of a fair and delicate make,
Most gently nurtured, to whom stripes and threats
And our foul prison-house were things undreamed.
But little by little as our spirits grew
Inured to suffering, with clasped hands, and tongues
That cheered each other to incessant prayer,
We rose and faced our trouble: we recalled
Our Master's sacred agony and death,
Setting before our eyes the high reward
Of steadfast faith, the martyr's deathless crown.

So passed some days whose length and count we lost,
Our bitterest trial. Then a respite came.
One who had interest with the governor
Wrought our removal daily for some hours
Into an upper chamber, where we sat
And held each other's hands in childish joy,
Receiving the sweet gift of light and air
With wonder and exceeding thankfulness.
And then began that life of daily growth
In mutual exaltation and sweet help
That bore us as a gently widening stream
Unto the ocean of our martyrdom.
Uniting all our feebler souls in one
A mightier - we reached forth with this to God.

Perpetua had been troubled for her babe,
Robbed of the breast and now these many days
Wasting for want of food; but when that change
Whereof I spake, of light and liberty
Relieved the horror of our prison gloom,
They brought it to her, and she sat apart,
And nursed and tended it, and soon the child
Would not be parted from her arms, but throve
And fattened, and she kept it night and day.
And always at her side with sleepless care
Hovered the young Felicitas - a slight
And spiritual figure - every touch and tone
Charged with premonitory tenderness,
Herself so near to her own motherhood.
Thus lightened and relieved, Perpetua
Recovered from her silent fit. Her eyes
Regained their former deep serenity,
Her tongue its gentle daring; for she knew
Her life should not be taken till her babe
Had strengthened and outgrown the need of her.

Daily we were amazed at her soft strength,
Her pliant and untroubled constancy,
Her smiling, soldierly contempt of death,
Her beauty and the sweetness of her voice.

Her father, when our first few bitterest days
Were over, like a gust of grief and rage,
Came to her in the prison with wild eyes,
And cried: 'How mean you, daughter, when you say
You are a Christian? How can any one
Of honoured blood, the child of such as me,
Be Christian? 'Tis an odious name, the badge
Only of outcasts and rebellious slaves!'
And she, grief-touched, but with unyielding gaze,
Showing the fulness of her slender height:
'This vessel, father, being what it is,
An earthen pitcher, would you call it thus?
Or would you name it by some other name?'
'Nay, surely,' said the old man, catching breath,
And pausing, and she answered: 'Nor can I
Call myself aught but what I surely am
A Christian!' and her father, flashing back
In silent anger, left her for that time.

A special favour to Perpetua
Seemed daily to be given, and her soul
Was made the frequent vessel of God's grace,
Wherefrom we all, less gifted, sore athirst,
Drank courage and fresh joy; for glowing dreams
Were sent her, full of forms august, and fraught
With signs and symbols of the glorious end
Whereto God's love hath aimed us for Christ's sake.
Once, at what hour I know not, for we lay
In that foul dungeon, where all hours were lost,
And day and night were indistinguishable
We had been sitting a long silent while,
Some lightly sleeping, others bowed in prayer,
When on a sudden, like a voice from God,
Perpetua spake to us and all were roused.
Her voice was rapt and solemn: 'Friends,' she said,
'Some word hath come to me in a dream. I saw
A ladder leading to heaven, all of gold,
Hung up with lances, swords, and hooks. A land
Of darkness and exceeding peril lay
Around it, and a dragon fierce as hell
Guarded its foot. We doubted who should first
Essay it, but you, Saturus, at last
So God hath marked you for especial grace
Advancing and against the cruel beast
Aiming the potent weapon of Christ's name
Mounted, and took me by the hand, and I
The next one following, and so the rest

In order, and we entered with great joy
Into a spacious garden filled with light
And balmy presences of love and rest;
And there an old man sat, smooth-browed, white-haired,
Surrounded by unnumbered myriads
Of spiritual shapes and faces angel-eyed,
Milking his sheep; and lifting up his eyes
He welcomed us in strange and beautiful speech,
Unknown yet comprehended, for it flowed
Not through the ears, but forth-right to the soul,
God's language of pure love. Between the lips
Of each he placed a morsel of sweet curd;
And while the curd was yet within my mouth,
I woke, and still the taste of it remains,
Through all my body flowing like white flame,
Sweet as of some immaculate spiritual thing.'
And when Perpetua had spoken, all
Were silent in the darkness, pondering,
But Saturus spake gently for the rest:
'How perfect and acceptable must be
Your soul to God, Perpetua, that thus
He bends to you, and through you speaks his will.
We know now that our martyrdom is fixed,
Nor need we vex us further for this life.'

While yet these thoughts were bright upon our souls,
There came the rumour that a day was set
To hear us. Many of our former friends,
Some with entreaties, some with taunts and threats,
Came to us to pervert us; with the rest
Again Perpetua's father, worn with care;
Nor could we choose but pity his distress,
So miserably, with abject cries and tears,
He fondled her and called her 'Domina,'
And bowed his agèd body at her feet,
Beseeching her by all the names she loved
To think of him, his fostering care, his years,
And also of her babe, whose life, he said,
Would fail without her; but Perpetua,
Sustaining by a gift of strength divine
The fulness of her noble fortitude,
Answered him tenderly: 'Both you and I,
And all of us, my father, at this hour
Are equally in God's hands, and what he wills
Must be'; but when the poor old man was gone
She wept, and knelt for many hours in prayer,
Sore tried and troubled by her tender heart.

One day, while we were at our midday meal,
Our cell was entered by the soldiery,
And we were seized and borne away for trial.
A surging crowd had gathered, and we passed

From street to street, hemmed in by tossing heads
And faces cold or cruel; yet we caught
At moments from masked lips and furtive eyes
Of friends, some known to as and some unknown
Many veiled messages of love and praise.
The floorways of the long basilica
Fronted us with an angry multitude;
And scornful eyes and threatening foreheads frowned
In hundreds from the columned galleries.
We were placed all together at the bar,
And though at first unsteadied and confused
By the imperial presence of the law,
The pomp of judgment and the staring crowd,
None failed or faltered; with unshaken tongue
Each met the stern Proconsul's brief demand
In clear profession. Rapt as in a dream,
Scarce conscious of my turn, nor how I spake,
I watched with wondering eyes the delicate face
And figure of Perpetua; for her
We that were youngest of our company
Loved with a sacred and absorbing love,
A passion that our martyr's brotherly vow
Had purified and made divine. She stood
In dreamy contemplation, slightly bowed,
A glowing stillness that was near a smile
Upon her soft closed lips. Her turn had come,
When, like a puppet struggling up the steps,
Her father from the pierced and swaying crowd
Appeared, unveiling in his agèd arms
The smiling visage of her babe. He grasped
Her robe, and strove to draw her down. All eyes
Were bent upon her. With a softening glance,
And voice less cold and heavy with death's doom,
The old Proconsul turned to her and said:
'Lady, have pity on your father's age;
Be mindful of your tender babe; this grain
Of harmless incense offer for the peace
And welfare of the Emperor'; but she,
Lifting far forth her large and noteless eyes,
As one that saw a vision, only said:
'I cannot sacrifice'; and he, harsh tongued,
Bending a brow upon her rough as rock,
With eyes that struck like steel, seeking to break
Or snare her with a sudden stroke of fear:
'Art thou a Christian?' and she answered, 'Yea,
I am a Christian!' In brow-blackening wrath
He motioned a contemptuous hand and bade
The lictors scourge the old man down and forth
With rods, and as the cruel deed was done,
Perpetua stood white with quivering lips,
And her eyes filled with tears. While yet his cries
Were mingling with the curses of the crowd,

Hilarianus, calling name by name,
Gave sentence, and in cold and formal phrase
Condemned us to the beasts, and we returned
Rejoicing to our prison. Then we wished
Our martyrdom could soon have followed, not
As doubting for our constancy, but some
Grew sick under the anxious long suspense.
Perpetua again was weighed upon
By grief and trouble for her babe, whom now
Her father, seeking to depress her will,
Withheld and would not send it; but at length
Word being brought her that the child indeed
No longer suffered, nor desired the breast,
Her peace returned, and, giving thanks to God,
All were united in new bonds of hope.
Now being fixed in certitude of death,
We stripped our souls of all their earthly gear,
The useless raiment of this world; and thus,
Striving together with a single will,
In daily increment of faith and power,
We were much comforted by heavenly dreams,
And waking visitations of God's grace.
Visions of light and glory infinite
Were frequent with us, and by night or day
Woke at the very name of Christ the Lord,
Taken at any moment on our lips;
So that we had no longer thought or care
Of life or of the living, but became
As spirits from this earth already freed,
Scarce conscious of the dwindling weight of flesh.
To Saturus appeared in dreams the space
And splendour of the heavenly house of God,
The glowing gardens of eternal joy,
The halls and chambers of the cherubim,
In wreaths of endless myriads involved
The blinding glory of the angel choir,
Rolling through deeps of wheeling cloud and light
The thunder of their vast antiphonies.
The visions of Perpetua not less
Possessed us with their homely tenderness
As one, wherein she saw a rock-set pool
And weeping o'er its rim a little child,
Her brother, long since dead, Dinocrates:
Though sore athirst, he could not reach the stream,
Being so small, and her heart grieved thereat.
She looked again, and lo! the pool had risen,
And the child filled his goblet, and drank deep,
And prattling in a tender childish joy
Ran gaily off, as infants do, to play.
By this she knew his soul had found release
From torment, and had entered into bliss.

Quickly as by a merciful gift of God,
Our vigil passed unbroken. Yesternight
They moved us to the amphitheatre,
Our final lodging-place on earth, and there
We sat together at our agapé
For the last time. In silence, rapt and pale,
We hearkened to the aged Saturus,
Whose speech, touched with a ghostly eloquence,
Canvassed the fraud and littleness of life,
God's goodness and the solemn joy of death.
Perpetua was silent, but her eyes
Fell gently upon each of us, suffused
With inward and eradiant light; a smile
Played often upon her lips.

While yet we sat,
A tribune with a band of soldiery
Entered our cell, and would have had us bound
In harsher durance, fearing our escape
By fraud or witchcraft; but Perpetua,
Facing him gently with a noble note
Of wonder in her voice, and on her lips
A lingering smile of mournful irony:
'Sir, are ye not unwise to harass us,
And rob us of our natural food and rest?
Should ye not rather tend us with soft care,
And so provide a comely spectacle?
We shall not honour Cæsar's birthday well,
If we be waste and weak, a piteous crew,
Poor playthings for your proud and pampered beasts.'
The noisy tribune, whether touched indeed,
Or by her grave and tender grace abashed,
Muttered and stormed a while, and then withdrew.
The short night passed in wakeful prayer for some,
For others in brief sleep, broken by dreams
And spiritual visitations. Earliest dawn
Found us arisen, and Perpetua,
Moving about with smiling lips, soft-tongued,
Besought us to take food; lest so, she said,
For all the strength and courage of our hearts,
Our bodies should fall faint. We heard without,
Already ere the morning light was full,
The din of preparation, and the hum
Of voices gathering in the upper tiers;
Yet had we seen so often in our thoughts
The picture of this strange and cruel death,
Its festal horror, and its bloody pomp,
The nearness scarcely moved us, and our hands
Met in a steadfast and unshaken clasp.

The day is over. Ah, my friend, how long
With its wild sounds and bloody sights it seemed!

Night comes, and I am still alive, even I,
The least and last, with other two, reserved
To grace to-morrow's second day. The rest
Have suffered and with holy rapture passed
Into their glory. Saturus and the men
Were given to bears and leopards, but the crowd
Feasted their eyes upon no cowering shape,
Nor hue of fear, nor painful cry. They died
Like armèd men, face foremost to the beasts,
With prayers and sacred songs upon their lips.
Perpetua and the frail Felicitas
Were seized before our eyes and roughly stripped,
And shrinking and entreating, not for fear,
Nor hurt, but bitter shame, were borne away
Into the vast arena, and hung up
In nets, naked before the multitude,
For a fierce bull, maddened by goads, to toss.
Some sudden tumult of compassion seized
The crowd, and a great murmur like a wave
Rose at the sight, and grew, and thundered up
From tier to tier, deep and imperious:
So white, so innocent they were, so pure:
Their tender limbs so eloquent of shame;
And so our loved ones were brought back, all faint,
And covered with light raiment, and again
Led forth, and now with smiling lips they passed
Pale, but unbowed, into the awful ring,
Holding each other proudly by the hand.

Perpetua first was tossed, and her robe rent,
But, conscious only of the glaring eyes,
She strove to hide herself as best she could
In the torn remnants of her flimsy robe,
And putting up her hands clasped back her hair,
So that she might not die as one in grief,
Unseemly and dishevelled. Then she turned,
And in her loving arms caressed and raised
The dying, bruised Felicitas. Once more
Gored by the cruel beast, they both were borne
Swooning and mortally stricken from the field.
Perpetua, pale and beautiful, her lips
Parted as in a lingering ecstasy,
Could not believe the end had come, but asked
When they were to be given to the beasts.
The keepers gathered round her, even they
In wondering pity, while with fearless hand,
Bidding us all be faithful and stand firm,
She bared her breast, and guided to its goal
The gladiator's sword that pierced her heart.

The night is passing. In a few short hours
I too shall suffer for the name of Christ.

A boundless exaltation lifts my soul!
I know that they who left us, Saturus,
Perpetua, and the other blessed ones,
Await me at the opening gates of heaven.

The Mystery Of A Year

A little while, a year agone,
I knew her for a romping child,
A dimple and a glance that shone
With idle mischief when she smiled.

To-day she passed me in the press,
And turning with a quick surprise
I wondered at her stateliness,
I wondered at her altered eyes.

To me the street was just the same,
The people and the city's stir;
But life had kindled into flame,
And all the world was changed for her.

I watched her in the crowded ways,
A noble form, a queenly head,
With all the woman in her gaze,
The conscious woman in her tread.

Winter Evening

To-night the very horses springing by
Toss gold from whitened nostrils. In a dream
The streets that narrow to the westward gleam
Like rows of golden palaces; and high
From all the crowded chimneys tower and die
A thousand aureoles. Down in the west
The brimming plains beneath the sunset rest,
One burning sea of gold. Soon, soon shall fly
The glorious vision, and the hours shall feel
A mightier master; soon from height to height,
With silence and the sharp unpitying stars,
Stern creeping frosts, and winds that touch like steel,
Out of the depth beyond the eastern bars,
Glittering and still shall come the awful night.

War

By the Nile, the sacred river,
I can see the captive hordes
Strain beneath the lash and quiver
At the long papyrus cords,
While in granite rapt and solemn,
Rising over roof and column,

Amen-hotep dreams, or Ramses,
Lord of Lords.

I can hear the trumpets waken
For a victory old and far
Carchemish or Kadesh taken
I can see the conqueror's car
Bearing down some Hittite valley,
Where the bowmen break and sally,
Sargina or Esarhaddon,
Grim with war!

From the mountain streams that sweeten
Indus, to the Spanish foam,
I can feel the broad earth beaten
By the serried tramp of Rome;
Through whatever foes environ
Onward with the might of iron
Veni, vidi; veni, vici
Crashing home!

I can see the kings grow pallid
With astonished fear and hate,
As the hosts of Amr or Khaled
On their cities fall like fate;
Like the heat-wind from its prison
In the desert burst and risen
La ilàha illah 'llàhu
God is great!

I can hear the iron rattle,
I can see the arrows sting
In some far-off northern battle,
Where the long swords sweep and swing;
I can hear the scalds declaiming,
I can see their eyeballs flaming,
Gathered in a frenzied circle
Round the king.

I can hear the horn of Uri
Roaring in the hills enorm;
Kindled at its brazen fury,
I can see the clansmen form;
In the dawn in misty masses,
Pouring from the silent passes
Over Granson or Morgarten
Like the storm.

On the lurid anvil ringing
To some slow fantastic plan,
I can hear the sword-smith singing
In the heart of old Japan

Till the cunning blade grows tragic
With his malice and his magic
Tenka tairan! Tenka tairan!
War to man!

Where a northern river charges
By a wild and moonlit glade,
From the murky forest marges,
Round a broken palisade,
I can see the red men leaping,
See the sword of Daulac sweeping,
And the ghostly forms of heroes
Fall and fade.

I can feel the modern thunder
Of the cannon beat and blaze,
When the lines of men go under
On your proudest battle-days;
Through the roar I hear the lifting
Of the bloody chorus drifting
Round the burning mill at Valmy
Marseillaise!

I can see the ocean rippled
With the driving shot like rain,
While the hulls are crushed and crippled,
And the guns are piled with slain;
O'er the blackened broad sea-meadow
Drifts a tall and titan shadow,
And the cannon of Trafalgar
Startle Spain.

Still the tides of fight are booming,
And the barren blood is spilt;
Still the banners are up-looming,
And the hands are on the hilt;
But the old world waxes wiser,
From behind the bolted visor
It descries at last the horror
And the guilt.

Yet the eyes are dim, nor wholly
Open to the golden gleam,
And the brute surrenders slowly
To the godhead and the dream.
From his cage of bar and girder,
Still at moments mad with murder,
Leaps the tiger, and his demon
Rules supreme.

One more war with fire and famine
Gathers, I can hear its cries

And the years of might and Mammon
Perish in a world's demise;
When the strength of man is shattered,
And the powers of earth are scattered,
From beneath the ghastly ruin
Peace shall rise!

The Woodcutter's Hut

Far up in the wild and wintery hills in the heart of the cliff-broken
woods,
Where the mounded drifts lie soft and deep in the noiseless solitudes,
The hut of the lonely woodcutter stands, a few rough beams that show
A blunted peak and a low black line, from the glittering waste of snow.
In the frost-still dawn from his roof goes up in the windless,
motionless air,
The thin, pink curl of leisurely smoke; through the forest white and
bare
The woodcutter follows his narrow trail, and the morning rings and
cracks
With the rhythmic jet of his sharp-blown breath and the echoing shout of
his axe.
Only the waft of the wind besides, or the stir of some hardy bird
The call of the friendly chickadee, or the pat of the nuthatch is
heard;
Or a rustle comes from a dusky clump, where the busy siskins feed,
And scatter the dimpled sheet of the snow with the shells of the
cedar-seed.
Day after day the woodcutter toils untiring with axe and wedge,
Till the jingling teams come up from the road that runs by the valley's
edge,
With plunging of horses, and hurling of snow, and many a shouted word,
And carry away the keen-scented fruit of his cutting, cord upon cord.
Not the sound of a living foot comes else, not a moving visitant there,
Save the delicate step of some halting doe, or the sniff of a prowling
bear.
And only the stars are above him at night, and the trees that creak and
groan,
And the frozen, hard-swept mountain-crests with their silent fronts of
stone,
As he watches the sinking glow of his fire and the wavering flames
upcaught,
Cleaning his rifle or mending his moccasins, sleepy and slow of
thought.
Or when the fierce snow comes, with the rising wind, from the grey
north-east,
He lies through the leaguering hours in his bunk like a winter-hidden
beast,
Or sits on the hard-packed earth, and smokes by his draught-blown
guttering fire,
Without thought or remembrance, hardly awake, and waits for the storm
to tire.

Scarcely he hears from the rock-rimmed heights to the wild ravines below,
Near and far-off, the limitless wings of the tempest hurl and go
In roaring gusts that plunge through the cracking forest, and lull, and lift,
All day without stint and all night long with the sweep of the hissing drift.
But winter shall pass ere long with its hills of snow and its fettered dreams,
And the forest shall glimmer with living gold, and chime with the gushing of streams;
Millions of little points of plants shall prick through its matted floor,
And the wind-flower lift and uncurl her silken buds by the woodman's door;
The sparrow shall see and exult; but lo! as the spring draws gaily on,
The woodcutter's hut is empty and bare, and the master that made it is gone.
He is gone where the gathering of valley men another labour yields,
To handle the plough, and the harrow, and scythe, in the heat of the summer fields.
He is gone with his corded arms, and his ruddy face, and his moccasined feet,
The animal man in his warmth and vigour, sound, and hard, and complete.
And all summer long, round the lonely hut, the black earth burgeons and breeds,
Till the spaces are filled with the tall-plumed ferns and the triumphing forest-weeds;
The thick wild raspberries hem its walls, and, stretching on either hand,
The red-ribbed stems and the giant-leaves of the sovereign spikenard stand.
So lonely and silent it is, so withered and warped with the sun and snow,
You would think it the fruit of some dead man's toil a hundred years ago;
And he who finds it suddenly there, as he wanders far and alone,
Is touched with a sweet and beautiful sense of something tender and gone,
The sense of a struggling life in the waste, and the mark of a soul's command,
The going and coming of vanished feet, the touch of a human hand.

Amor Vitae
I love the warm bare earth and all
That works and dreams thereon:
I love the seasons yet to fall:
I love the ages gone,

The valleys with the sheeted grain,
The river's smiling might,

The merry wind, the rustling rain,
The vastness of the night.

I love the morning's flame, the steep
Where down the vapour clings:
I love the clouds that float and sleep,
And every bird that sings.

I love the purple shower that pours
On far-off fields at even:
I love the pine-wood dusk whose floors
Are like the courts of heaven.

I love the heaven's azure span,
The grass beneath my feet:
I love the face of every man
Whose thought is swift and sweet.

I let the wrangling world go by,
And like an idle breath
Its echoes and its phantoms fly:
I care no jot for death.

Time like a Titan bright and strong
Spreads one enchanted gleam:
Each hour is but a fluted song,
And life a lofty dream.

Winter Break
All day between high-curded clouds the sun
Shone down like summer on the steaming planks.
The long, bright icicles in dwindling ranks
Dripped from the murmuring eaves till one by one
They fell. As if the spring had now begun,
The quilted snow, sun-softened to the core,
Loosened and shunted with a sudden roar
From downward roofs. Not even with day done
Had ceased the sound of waters, but all night
I heard it. In my dreams forgetfully bright
Methought I wandered in the April woods,
Where many a silver-piping sparrow was,
By gurgling brooks and spouting solitudes,
And stooped, and laughed, and plucked hepaticas.